brush

floss

flush

wash

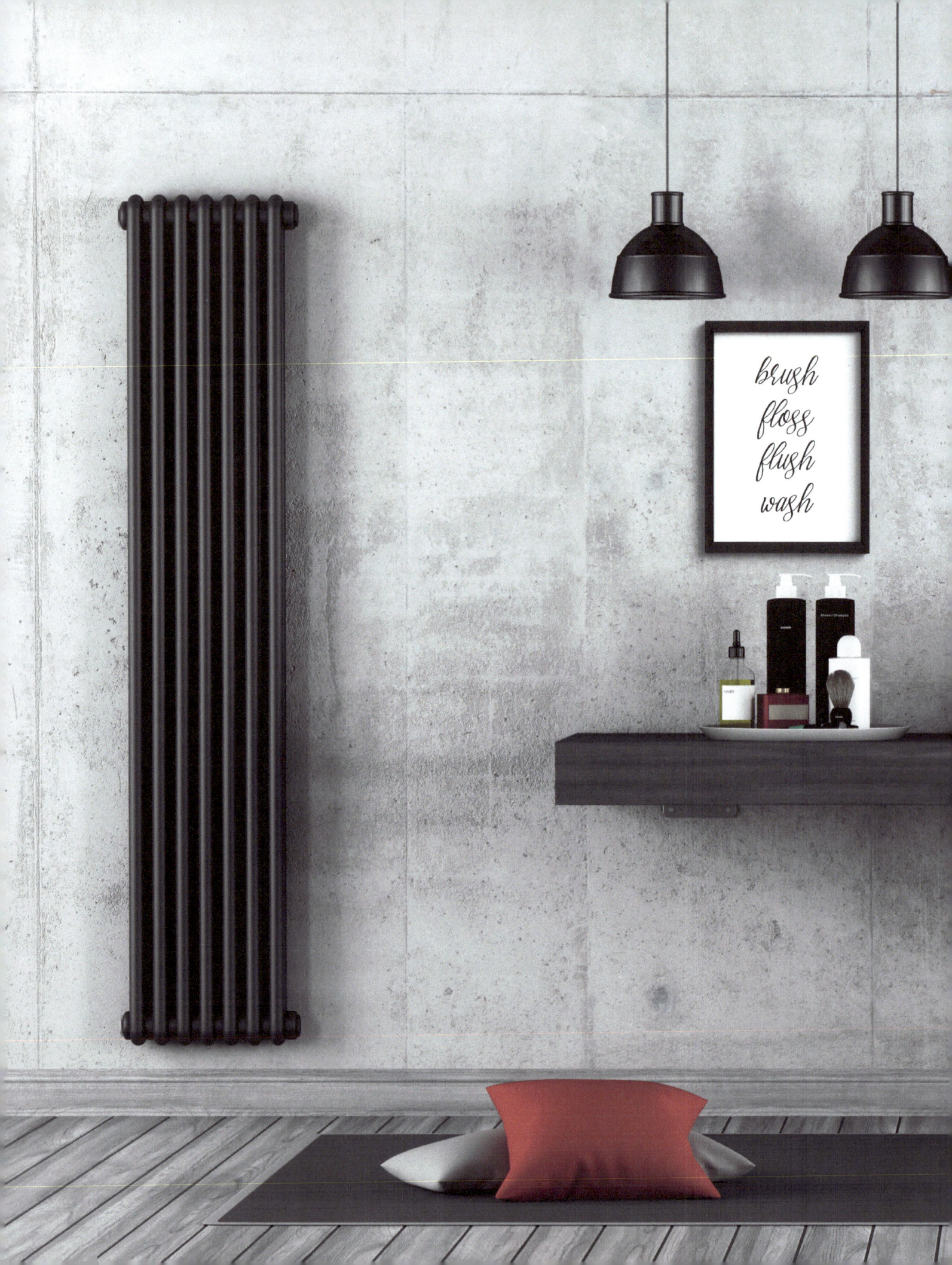

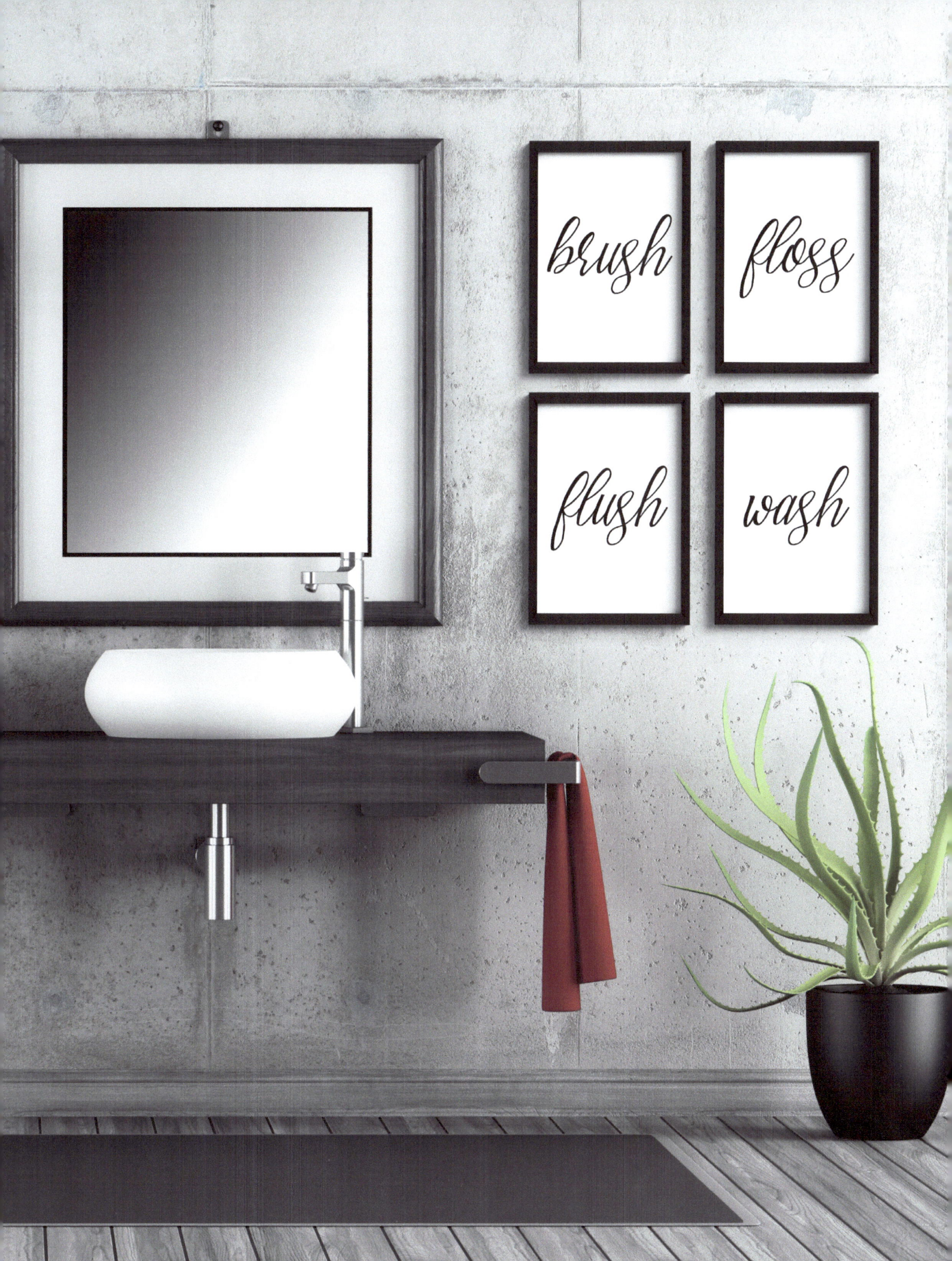

Step 1: Cut the illustrations out of the book.

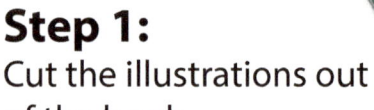

Step 2: Frame the illustrations.

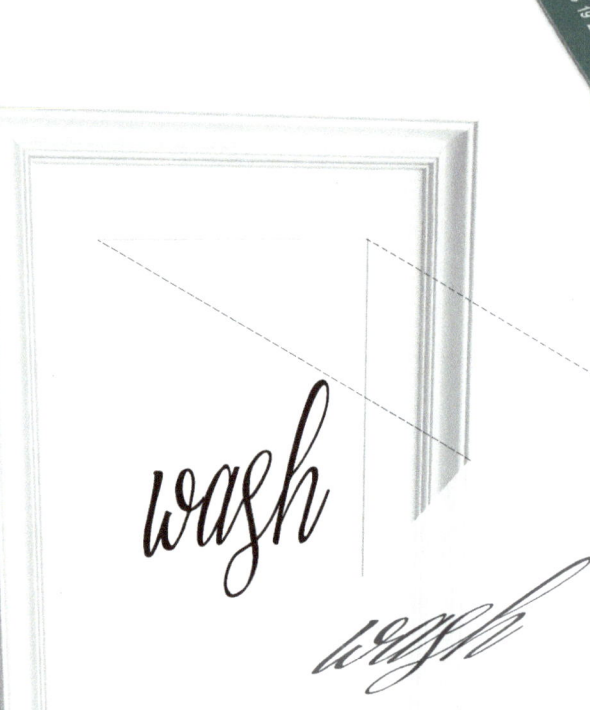

Step 3: Hang them on the wall and enjoy!

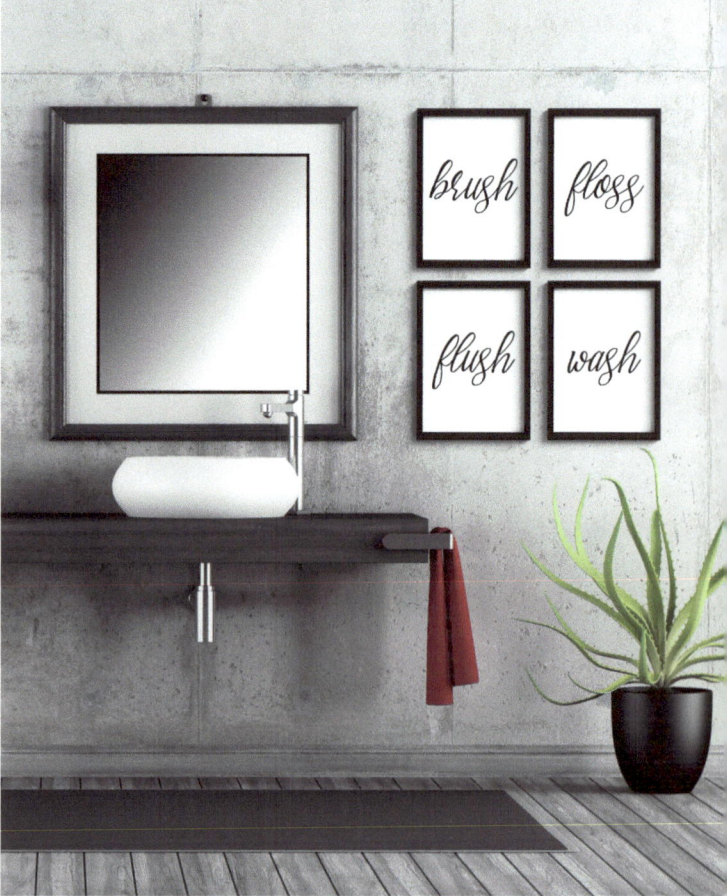

INSTRUCTIONS

· Cut out and frame the pages for an outstanding wall decoration.
· The page size is 8.5x11" providing you an extra white border and guide lines for easy cutting and framing.
· Perfect for 8x10" frames.
· Frames are not included.

INTERESTING

· Perfect for any room of the house!
· High-quality art print.
· Exceptional contrast and color saturation.

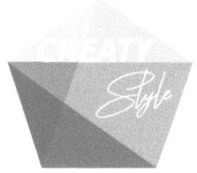

Copyright © 2021 Creaty Style

All rights reserved. This book or any portion thereof may not be reproduced or used in any manner whatsoever without the express written permission of the publiser.

www.creatystyle.com

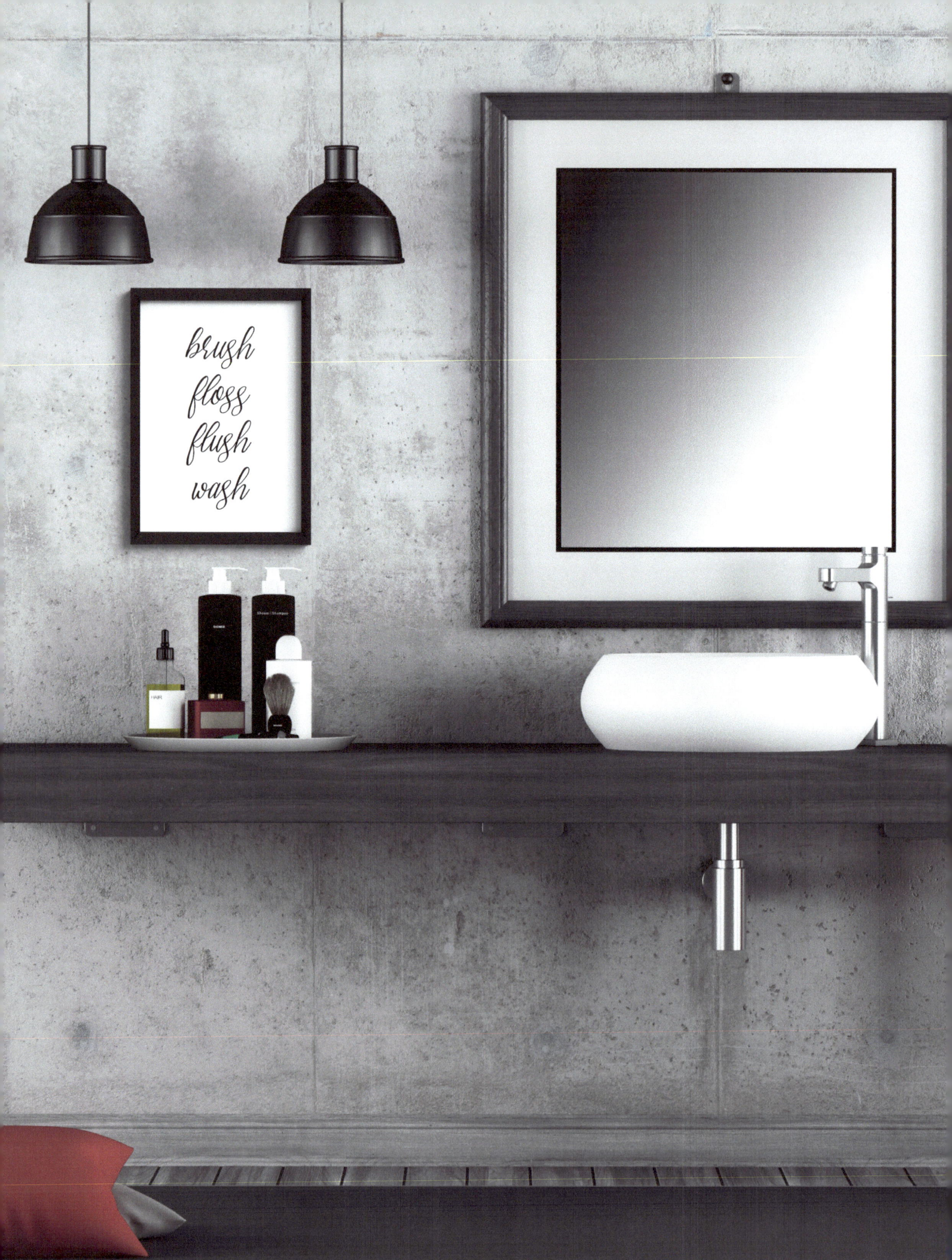

brush

floss

flush

wash

brush

floss

flush

wash

A little 5x7" present for you...

brush

floss

flush

wash

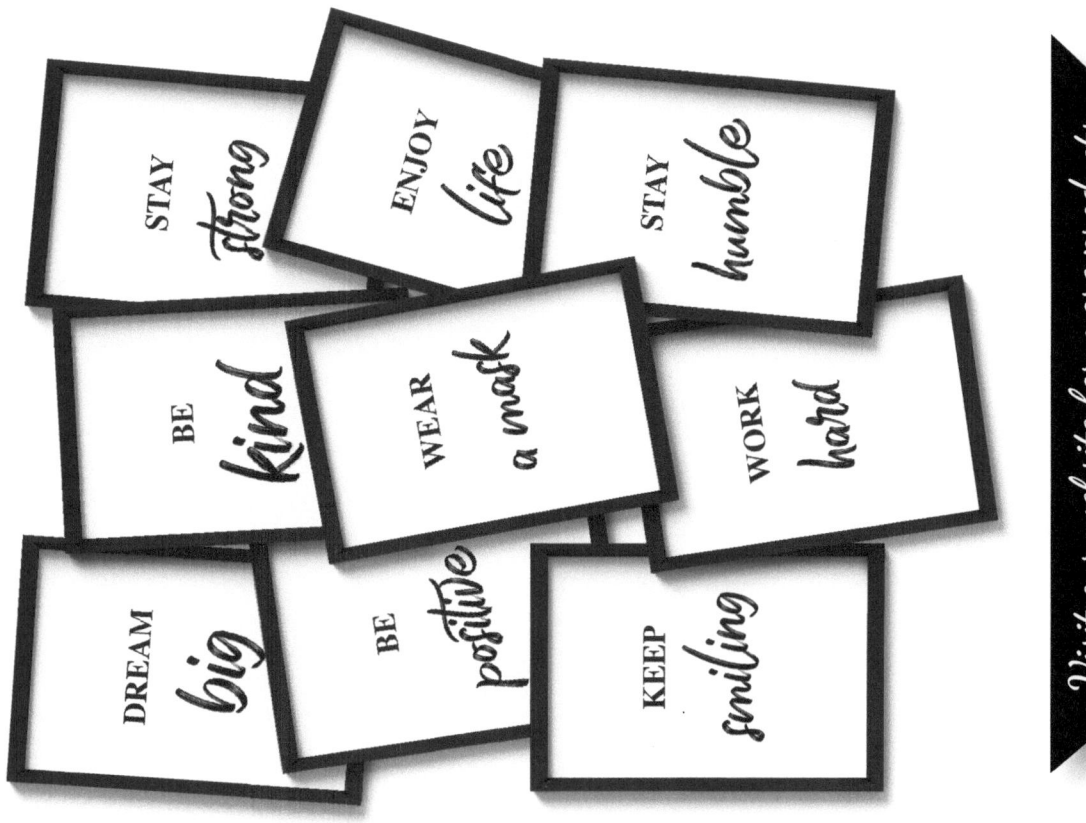

brush

floss

flush

wash

www.ingramcontent.com/pod-product-compliance
Lightning Source LLC
Chambersburg PA
CBHW051839210526
45473CB00005B/1947